I Am Growing *Every Day!*

A Reflection & Growth Journal for Children

Ages 5-8

By

Valerie J. Lewis Coleman

Published by

Pen of the Writer, LLC
Englewood, Ohio
PenOfTheWriter.com

Published by

Pen of the Writer, LLC
Englewood, Ohio
PenOfTheWriter.com

ISBN: 979-8-9865108-4-2

Illustrations and cover design by Vladimir Cebu, LL.B.

Printed in the United States of America

This journal is designed to encourage self-expression and reflection. It is not intended to replace professional medical, psychological, or educational advice.

Welcome!

This Journal Belongs To:

____

Growing takes time.

Sometimes you grow when you learn something new.

Sometimes you grow when you make a mistake.

Sometimes you grow just by trying.

This journal will help you notice that you are growing every day.

Put your special sticker here

My Growing Sticker

This journal was made just for me.

Why Your Story Matters

Your story is special because it belongs to *you*.

The way you think.

The way you feel.

The things you like and love.

The things you are learning.

All of it matters.

Writing helps you:

- Learn about your feelings
- Share your thoughts
- Try new ideas
- See how you are growing

You can use this journal in your own way. There is no right or wrong. You don't have to be perfect.

Just be you. Your voice matters—and your story is important.

A Note for Parents, Teachers, and Facilitators

Your child is about to begin a powerful journey of self-discovery. Some pages repeat throughout the journal because young children grow through repetition. When children return to the same prompts, they often:

- Express new ideas
- Use different words
- Draw with more confidence
- See themselves in new ways

There are no right or wrong answers in this journal.

Children may:

- Write on one page and draw on another
- Use stickers some days and not others
- Skip pages and return to them later

We encourage you to:

- Read prompts aloud
- Invite conversation
- Celebrate effort, not perfection
- Allow children to respond at their own pace

Every page is an invitation for children to reflect, dream, and discover the amazing person they already are. Each time a child revisits a page, they practice something powerful—seeing themselves as capable, growing, and full of potential. Encourage your child to write freely, draw boldly, and return to these pages again and again.

Look for ★ moments—these are great opportunities to invite your child to share their thoughts with you.

About When I See Me™

When I See Me™ is a literacy and confidence-building initiative created to help children see themselves as capable, valued, and worthy of greatness. Through books, journals, book fairs, and creative experiences, children are encouraged to explore their feelings, express their ideas, and discover the power of their own voices.

Each When I See Me™ journal supports emotional growth, self-awareness, and imagination while affirming a child's identity and potential. The activities inside invite children to reflect, create, and grow in ways that feel safe, engaging, and fun.

Through the When I See Me™ Children's Book Fairs, this mission comes to life in communities—placing diverse, empowering books directly into children's hands and creating experiences where they can meet authors, engage in meaningful activities, and see themselves as readers, writers, and leaders.

At its heart, When I See Me™ is about representation, encouragement, and helping every child believe:

"I matter. My voice matters. My story matters."

Learn more at **WhenISeeMe.com.**

Now, let's jump back in—there's something special waiting for you.

Meet Your When I See Me™ Friends

Now it's your turn. Before you begin, let's meet some friends who will be on this journey with you. They're discovering who they are—just like you.

Lyric, **Shawn**, **Nia**, **Samara**, and **Zoe** are here to cheer you on. They'll help you believe in yourself, understand your feelings, and use your voice with confidence. Every day, they're learning and growing—just like you.

I'm Lyric.

I love being me and showing up with confidence and joy.

Even on the days you forget, I remind you—something special is inside you.

I am amazing just the way I am.

I'm Shawn.

I believe growth takes time, and every step matters. I keep trying, even when things feel hard.

I remind you that mistakes help you learn and grow stronger every day.

I grow and learn every day.

I'm Nia.

I help make space for big feelings and gentle moments. I take time to understand what's happening inside my heart.

I remind you that every emotion has a purpose—and it's okay to feel them all.

All my feelings are welcome.

I'm Samara.

I use my voice to share ideas, lead, and encourage others. I'm not afraid to speak up and share what's on my mind.

I remind you that your voice matters—and what you say is important.

My voice matters.

I'm Zoe.

I love stories and turning ideas into something magical. I imagine, create, and express myself in my own unique way.

I remind you that your ideas are powerful and your creativity shines brightly.

I can create my own story.

Which When I See Me™ friend are you today?

Meet Shawn

Hi, I'm Shawn. I'm learning and growing every day—just like you! Sometimes things feel hard, but I don't give up. I try again, ask for help, and do my best. I'm here to remind you that growing takes time. Every step you take matters. Let's grow together.

What colors will you choose to show how you're growing?

I Am Growing When I...

I am growing when I _______________________________

____

Draw, write, or use a sticker to show yourself
learning or practicing something new.

All About Me

My name is _______________________________

I am _______________________ years old.

One thing I love to do is _______________________________

Draw yourself doing something you love.

⭐ *Tell someone what you love about yourself.*

I Try Again

Sometimes I don't get it right the first time. That's okay!

Something I tried again:

____

____

____

Draw, write, or use a sticker to show how you felt when you kept going.

I am still growing!

I Can Do Hard Things

Something I learned to do:

____

Draw, write, or use a sticker to show what you learned
and how you felt when you didn't give up.

What helped you not give up? _____________________________

____

____

Shawn believes in you as you grow.

Let's see how you are growing.

I Am Growing!

Something I'm getting better at:

____

Each step shows how you are growing. Draw yourself on the top step to celebrate how far you've come.

You may add a sticker that shows how you feel as you grow.

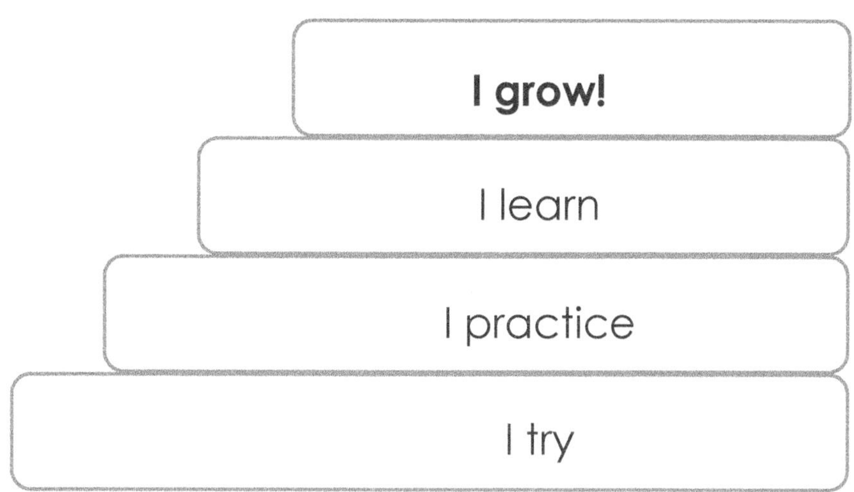

⭐ *Tell someone which step you are working on today.*

Kind Words About Me

These are kind words I can say about myself:

I am trying.

I am learning.

I am getting better.

Say these words out loud. You may trace them if you want.

One more kind word about me is:

____

You may add a sticker that reminds you of how special you are.

You Are Growing!

Circle, color, or mark **all** that help you grow.

☐ Trying again

☐ Asking for help

☐ Practicing

☐ Being kind

☐ Taking a break

Add a sticker or two to show how growing feels today.

⭐ *Tell someone what helps you when things feel hard.*

I Grow As I...

Circle **all** that are true for you. I grow as I

- ☐ try something new

- ☐ practice

- ☐ ask for help

- ☐ keep going

Finish the sentence:

I grow as I ____

I grow as I ____

I grow as I ____

Draw, write, or use a sticker to show yourself
growing while doing one of these things.

Oops...I Learned!

Something I didn't get right at first:

What I learned:

Draw, write, or use a sticker to show
how you felt when you kept going.

I Try Again

Sometimes I don't get it right the first time. That's okay!

Something I tried again:

____

____

____

Draw, write, or use a sticker to show when you kept going.

I am still growing!

⭐ *Tell someone how you felt when you didn't give up.*

I Can Do Hard Things

Something I learned to do:

____

Draw, write, or use a sticker

to show how you felt when you didn't give up.

What helped you not give up? _______________________

____

____

Take a break and color with Shawn.

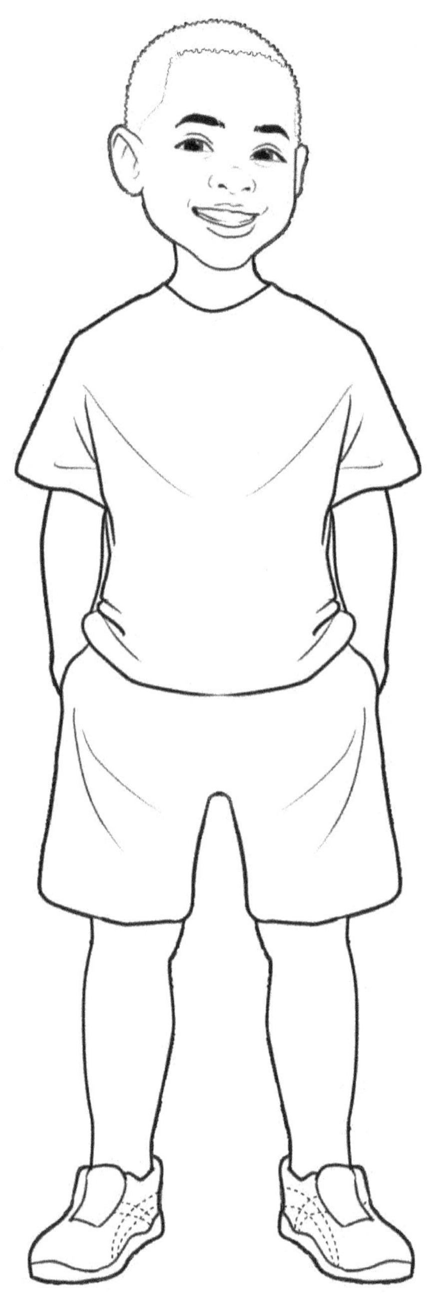

I Am Growing!

I'm getting better at:

____

Each step shows how you are growing. Draw yourself on the top step to celebrate how far you've come.

You may add a sticker that shows how you feel as you grow.

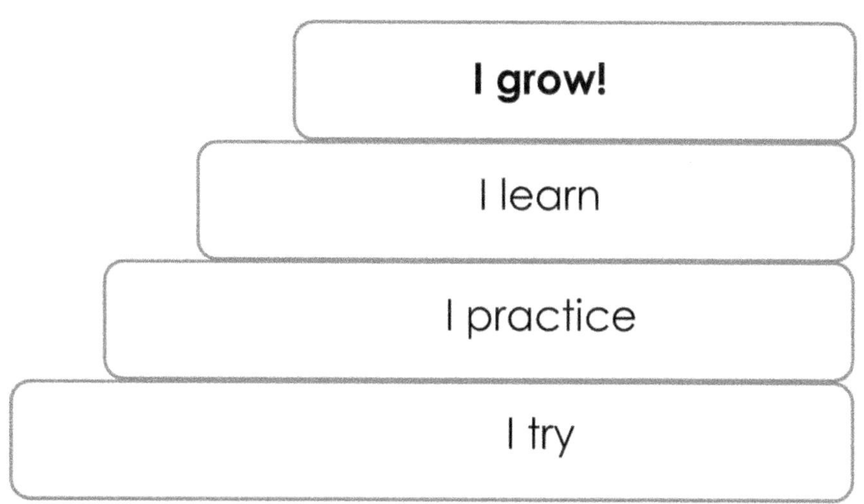

⭐ *Tell someone which step you are working on today.*

How Growth Feels

Circle, color, or mark **all** that match how you feel. Today, growing feels like:

☺ Happy

😵 Confused

😣 Frustrated

😌 Proud

Why do I feel this way?

____

____

____

Circle, color, or place a sticker.

⭐ *Tell someone about a feeling you had today.*

Look How I've Grown!

Before, I couldn't:

____

Now, I can:

____

Draw yourself before and after.

I Kept Going!

Something that was hard:

____

What helped me keep going?

- ☐ I asked for help.
- ☐ I practiced.
- ☐ I took a break.
- ☐ I tried again.

Add a sticker to celebrate yourself!

I Am Growing When I...

I am growing when I _______________________________

____

Draw, write, or use a sticker to show yourself
learning or practicing something new.

What I Learned About Me

As I grow, I learn new things about myself.

I learned that I am ______________________________

I learned that I can ______________________________

I learned that I feel proud when ______________________________

Draw, write, or use a sticker to show yourself
doing something that made you feel proud.

Circle **all** that are true for you:

I am proud of me.

I am still learning.

I will keep growing.

I am learning more about me every day!

I Try Again

Sometimes I don't get it right the first time. That's okay!

Something I tried again:

____

____

____

Draw, write, or use a sticker to show how you felt when you kept going.

I am still growing!

I Can Do Hard Things

Something I learned to do:

____

Draw, write, or use a sticker to show what you learned and
how you felt when you didn't give up.

What helped you not give up? _______________________________

____

____

Color Shawn being his amazing, growing self.

I Am Growing!

Something I'm getting better at:

____

Each step shows how you are growing. Draw yourself on the top step to celebrate how far you've come.

You may add a sticker that shows how you feel as you grow.

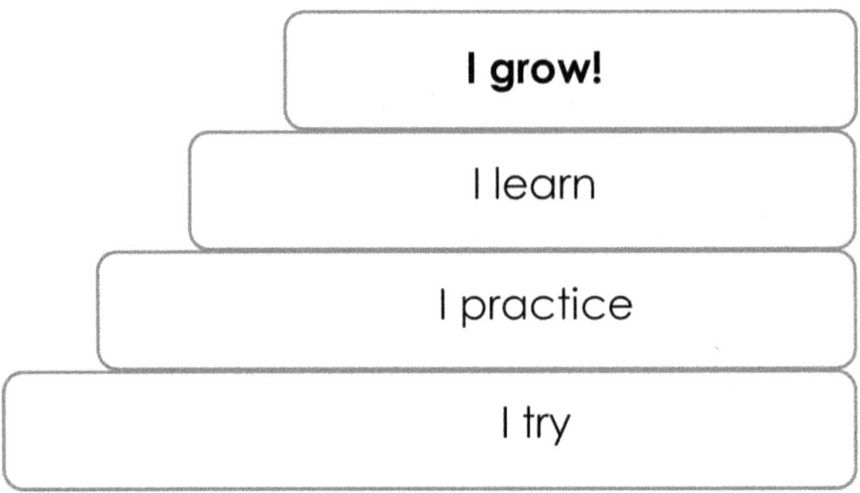

Kind Words About Me

These are kind words I can say about myself:

I am helpful.

I am thoughtful.

I am trying my best.

Say these words out loud. You may trace them if you want.

One more kind word about me is:

____

You may add a sticker that reminds you of how special you are.

Oops...I Learned!

Something I didn't get right at first:

____

____

What I learned:

____

____

Draw, write, or use a sticker to show what you would do next time.

I Grow As I...

Circle **all** that are true for you. I grow as I

- ☐ try something new
- ☐ practice
- ☐ ask for help
- ☐ keep going

Finish the sentence:

I grow as I ____

I grow as I ____

I grow as I ____

Draw, write, or use a sticker to show yourself growing
while doing one of these things.

⭐ *Tell someone how you are growing right now.*

Something I Do Well

One thing I do well is: _______________________________________

I am learning to: _______________________________________

Draw, write, or use a sticker to show yourself doing something well.

I Try Again

Sometimes I don't get it right the first time. That's okay!

Something I tried again:

____

____

Draw, write, or use a sticker to show how you felt when you kept going.

I am still growing!

I Can Do Hard Things

Something I learned to do:

____

Draw, write, or use a sticker
to show how you felt when you didn't give up.

What helped you not give up? _______________

____

____

Color and relax.

I Am Growing!

Something I'm getting better at:

____

Each step shows how you are growing. Draw yourself on the top step to celebrate how far you've come.

You may add a sticker that shows how you feel as you grow.

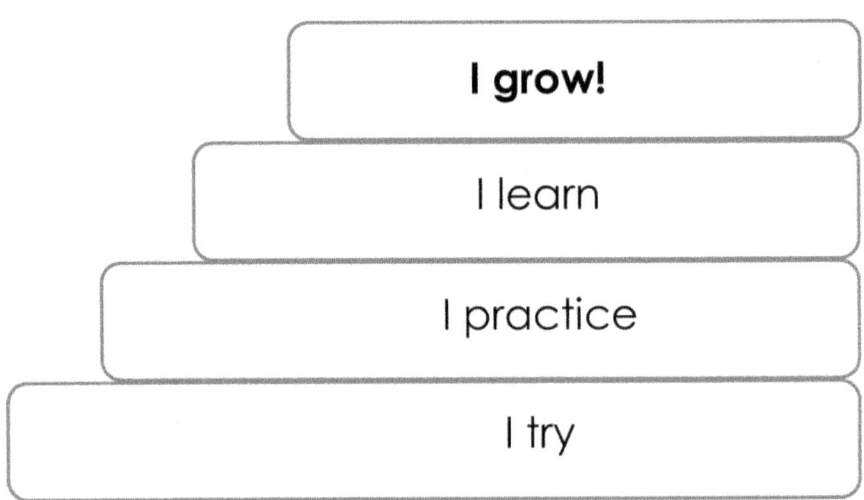

Look How I've Grown!

Before, I couldn't:

Now, I can:

Draw yourself before and after.

How Growth Feels

Circle, color, or mark **all** that match how you feel. Today, growing feels like:

😊 Happy

😵 Confused

😤 Frustrated

😌 Proud

Why do I feel this way?

____

____

____

Circle, color, or place a sticker.

I Am Growing When I...

I am growing when I _______________________________

____

Draw, write, or use a sticker to show yourself
learning or practicing something new.

I Kept Going!

Something that was hard:

____

What helped me keep going?

- ☐ I asked for help.
- ☐ I practiced.
- ☐ I took a break.
- ☐ I tried again.

Add a sticker to celebrate yourself!

I Try Again

Sometimes I don't get it right the first time. That's okay!

Something I tried again:

____

____

____

Draw, write, or use a sticker to show how you felt when you kept going.

I am still growing!

I Can Do Hard Things

Something I learned to do:

____

Draw, write, or use a sticker to show what you learned
when you didn't give up.

What helped you not give up? _______________________

I Am Growing!

Something I'm getting better at:

____

Each step shows how you are growing. Draw yourself on the top step to celebrate how far you've come.

You may add a sticker that shows how you feel as you grow.

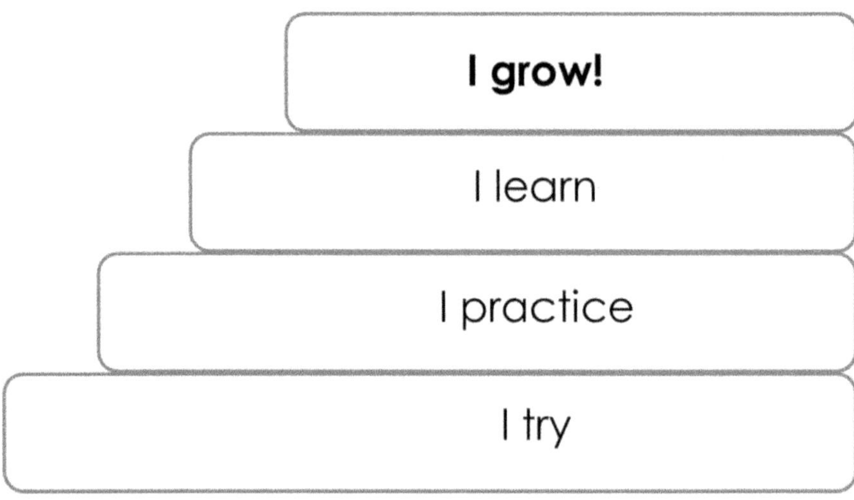

What I Learned About Me

As I grow, I learn new things about myself.

I learned that I am ____

I learned that I can ____

I learned that I feel proud when __________________________________

Draw, write, or use a sticker to show how you feel about what you learned.

Circle **all** that are true for you:

I am proud of me.

I am still learning.

I will keep growing.

I am learning more about me every day!

Oops...I Learned!

Something I didn't get right at first:

____

____

What I learned:

____

____

Draw, write, or use a sticker to show what you would do next time.

⭐ *Tell someone what you would try differently next time.*

I Am Growing When I...

I am growing when I ____________________________________

____

Draw, write, or use a sticker of yourself learning or practicing something new.

What Makes Me, Me

Something special about me is: _______________________________________

Something I like about myself is: _______________________________________

Draw, write, or use a sticker to show yourself.

I Try Again

Sometimes I don't get it right the first time. That's okay!

Something I tried again:

Draw, write, or use a sticker to show how you felt when you kept going.

I am still growing!

I Can Do Hard Things

Something I learned to do:

____

Draw, write, or use a sticker

to show how you felt when you didn't give up.

What helped you not give up? _______________________

____

____

Take a quiet moment and color Shawn.

I Am Growing!

Something I'm getting better at:

____

Each step shows how you are growing. Draw yourself on the top step to celebrate how far you've come.

You may add a sticker that shows how you feel as you grow.

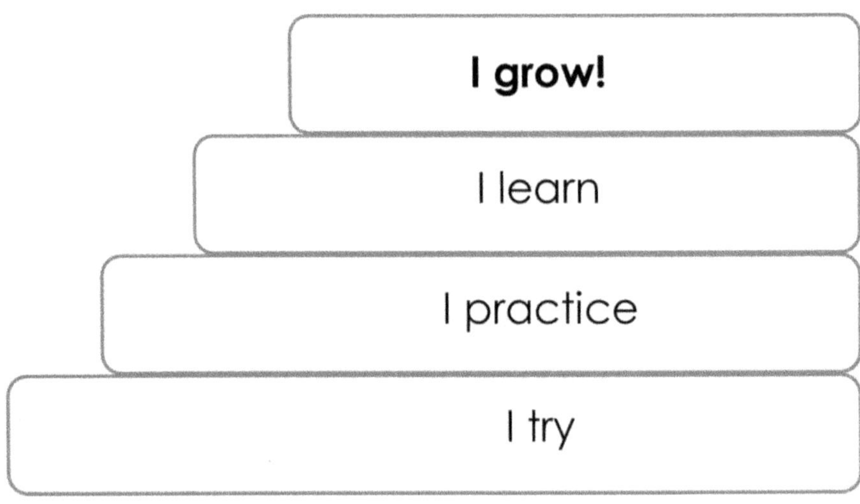

Kind Words About Me

These are kind words I can say about myself:

I am learning and growing.

I matter every day.

I am loved.

Say these words out loud. You may trace them if you want.

One more kind word about me is:

____

You may add a sticker that reminds you of how special you are.

How Growth Feels

Circle, color, or mark **all** that match how you feel. Today, growing feels like:

☺ Happy

☺ Confused

☺ Frustrated

☺ Proud

Why do I feel this way?

____

____

____

Circle, color, or place a sticker.

I Am Proud of My Growth

I am proud of myself because

Something I can do now:

Draw yourself celebrating.

Take a Moment

Draw, write, or use a sticker.

Something I want to remember is:

★ Tell someone one way you've grown.

Draw, write, or create anything you want here.

Your ideas matter.

When I Need Encouragement

Write, draw, or use a sticker to show what you say to yourself when things feel hard.

Share Your Words with Us

We'd love to see how you're using your journal!

With help from a parent or teacher, you can:

- Share a favorite page
- Show a drawing or reflection
- Tell us what you learned

Your voice matters. We'd love to celebrate your ideas!

Tag us @PenOfTheWriter

or share with #WhenISeeMe

Scan the code below to post in our Facebook group.

WhenISeeMe.com

Your words matter.

Growing takes time.

Growing takes effort.

And growing is something to be proud of.

You are growing every day.